ROCKS AND MINERALS

ROCKS AND MINERALS

CHARTWELL
BOOKS, INC.

Published by Chartwell Books
A Division of Book Sales Inc.
114 Northfield Avenue
Edison, New Jersey 08837
USA

Copyright ©1998 Quantum Books Ltd

ISBN 0-7858-0971-6

This book is produced by
Quantum Books Ltd
6 Blundell Street
London N7 9BH

Project Manager: Rebecca Kingsley
Project Editor: Judith Millidge
Design/Editorial: David Manson
Andy McColm, Maggie Manson

The material in this publication previously appeared in
Rocks, Shells, Fossils, Minerals and Gems,
Crystal Identifier, *The Gem and Mineral Collection*

QUMSPRM
Set in Futura
Reproduced in Singapore by Eray Scan
Printed in Singapore by Star Standard Industries (Pte) Ltd

Contents

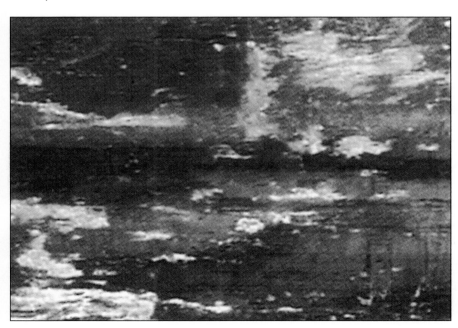

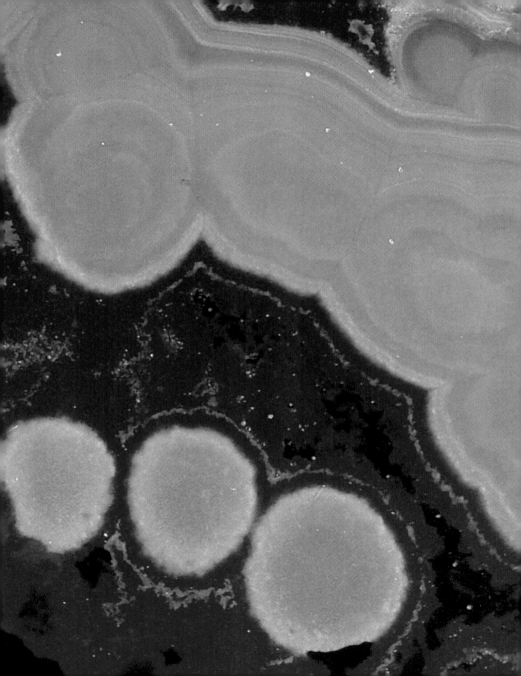

AMAZING ROCKS AND MINERALS

Rocks and minerals are basic fundamental components of the earth beneath our feet. There are approximately 3000 different forms. Some have always been valued for their beauty and rarity whilst others have a more straightforward structural function. However, the resourcefulness of man has meant that appropriate uses have been found for them all at some point in history.

Solid Rock Forms

Rocks, essentially, are collections of different minerals in solid form, although some consist of just one mineral, such as limestone and sandstone. There are three types of rocks: sedimentary, igneous and metamorphic.

SEDIMENTARY ROCKS

Sedimentary rocks are generally stratified, fine-grained or made of fragments of older rocks from which these were derived, such as pebbles, sand, broken shells, older rocks, rounded mineral grains and alteration minerals such as clays.

IGNEOUS ROCKS

Igneous rocks are non-stratified intrusions or extrusions. They can be very coarse-grained such as granite, fine-grained such as andesite, or glassy-grained such as obsidian. They are composed of minerals that have crystallized from molten rocks.

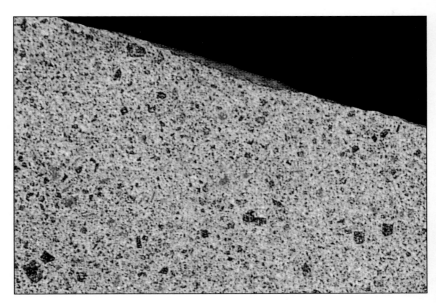

Left. Andesite is an example of a fine-grained igneous rock found in lava flows.

Above. Gneiss is a metamorphic rock found in the roots of mountain ranges.

METAMORPHIC ROCKS

Metamorphic rocks are made from sedimentary and igneous rocks which have been altered by heat and/or pressure. As they are derived from previously existing igneous, sedimentary and even some metamorphic rocks, their appearance is variable. They are generally identified by the types of minerals which they contain and their texture.

Thermally metamorphosed rocks border igneous intrusions, which altered many of the surrounding rocks originally because of their intense heat, resulting also in the formation of new minerals such as andalusite and garnet. Regionally metamorphosed rocks occur in the roots of mountain ranges, where intense pressures and very high temperatures formed many platy and high-pressure minerals.

Rock Properties

Field specimens of rocks are identified according to their composition, texture and mode of origin. Each major rock type has its own range of textures.

SEDIMENTARY TEXTURES

Clastic. Consisting of broken and weathered fragments of pre-existing rocks and/or minerals and/or shells, clastic rocks may have their individual components cemented together by calcite or iron oxide.

Crystalline. Consisting of crystals that have been precipitated from solution which are locked together.

Organic. Mainly composed of well-preserved organic debris such as plants, shells or bones.

IGNEOUS TEXTURES

Granular. Crystal grains that are large enough to be seen by the naked eye varying in size.

Aphanitic. Tiny crystals which can only be seen under a glass.

Glassy. Volcanic glass with micro crystals.

Pyroclastic. Fractured rocks with tiny slivers of volcanic glass.

Porphyritic. Larger crystals – phenocrysts – are embedded in a finer ground mass.

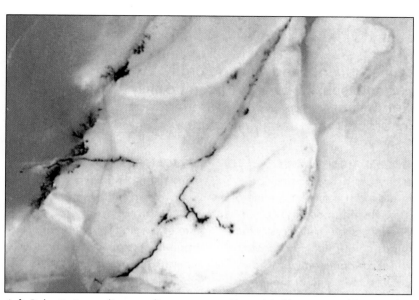

Left. Dolomite is a sedimentary limestone rock with crystalline deposits of gypsum.

Above. Marble is a granoblastic rock, banded and veined with various colors.

METAMORPHIC TEXTURES

Slaty. Finely crystalline rock in which minerals aligned in parallel allow the rock to split readily along cleavage planes, e.g. slate.

Schistose. Minerals are aligned in easily visible parallel bands allowing the rock to split easily.

Gneissose. Characterized by a coarse foliation with individual bands several centimetres across – it may even wrap around larger crystals – and all the minerals are coarsely granular and readily identifiable, e.g. gneiss.

Granoblastic. Mainly large mineral grains that may have crystallized at the same time and therefore penetrated each other, the grains remain large enough to be identified easily, such as marble.

Hornfels. Compact, finely grained rock that shatters into angular fragments.

THROUGHOUT THE DIRECTORY
The symbols which accompany each rock are commonly used to represent the rock-type on a geological map.

Mineral Structures

A mineral is defined as a naturally formed, solid, inorganic substance with a composition that is either fixed or that varies within a defined range, and within a characteristic atomic structure.

MINERAL PROPERTIES

The characteristic composition and atomic structure of a mineral are expressed in its physical properties, such as its crystalline form, its color and its hardness, In order to identify minerals and to understand some of the terms in the book, it is important to look at the way in which crystals are formed and defined.

CRYSTAL SYSTEMS

Many minerals have a crystalline structure and although it may be unusual for perfect crystals to form under natural conditions, the shape of crystals in a sample of mineral will give a collector a valuable clue to its identity. If a mineral is made up of a mass of small, poorly formed crystals it is termed **massive**.

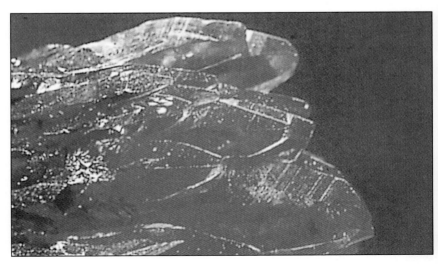

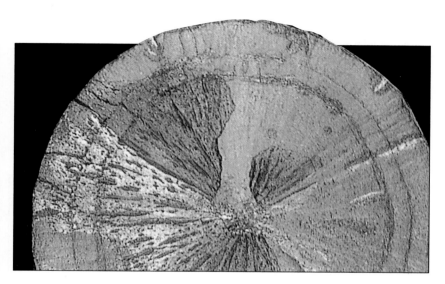

Left. Rhodochrosite is a massive, rose-red colored rhombohedral crystal.

Above. Pyrite is easily identified by its brassy gold color.

HABITS, FORMS AND FACES

The **habit** of a crystal is the usual shape it takes. The habit can be described as one or more of the crystal **forms** defined by sets of parallel faces and their angles. A form is made up of a number of identical faces and is termed a "closed form" if it can enclose space or an "open form" if it cannot. A crystal has a variety of **faces**, each of which is given a number according to the axes intersecting it. These **axes** form the basis of crystal classification (see p.14).

COLOR

Some colors are striking and serve a diagnostic purpose, while others are of lesser value. Minerals with characteristic color include malachite (green) and pyrite (yellow brassy gold).

LUSTER

Luster describes the way in which light is reflected off the surface of a mineral. Terms used: metallic, adamantine (brilliant), vitreous (broken glass), resinous, pearly, silky, splendent (reflective), shining, glistening and glimmering.

Crystal Systems

If you rotate a sugar cube about an axis running straight through the middle of two opposite faces, four identical square sides can be seen, one after another. A cube is said to have three axes of four-fold symmetry. These axes form the basis of classification of crystals.

Mineral Crystal Classification System

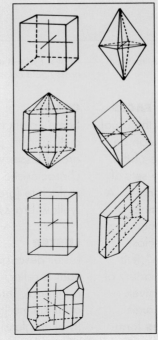

Isometric. All three axes are the same length and at right angles.

Tetragonal. Three right angled axes, two in the same plane and the third perpendicular.

Hexagonal. Of four axes, three in one plane and the fourth perpendicular.

Trigonal. Three axes at 60° in the same plane and the fourth is perpendicular.

Orthorhombic. Three unequal length axes, two at right angles.

Monoclinic. Three unequal axes, two at an oblique angle and the third perpendicular.

Triclinic. Three unequal length axes at different angles.

How to Use this Book

The information in the directory is arranged to supply the reader with a snapshot of information about each rock and mineral. A number of key icons are used throughout the book to reinforce the information visually. These are explained below.

Rocks and Mineral Uses

 Construction and building industry

 Industry and manufacturing

 Monuments and stone-masonry

 Science and technology

 Gemstones and jewels

 Fossils and collections

 Ornamental sculpture

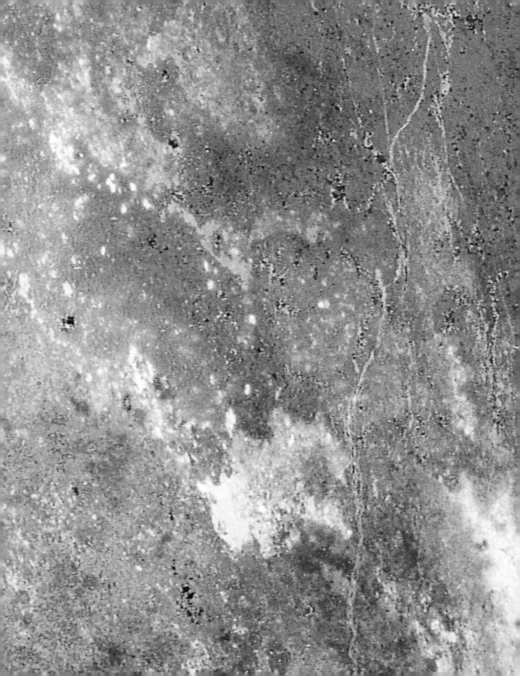

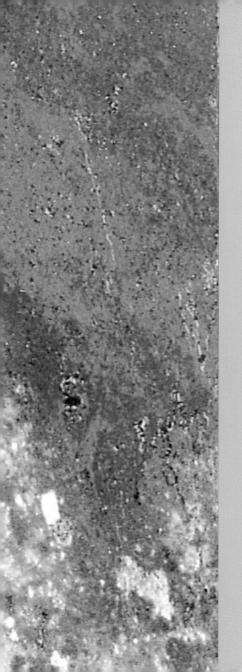

ROCK AND MINERAL SPECIMENS

CONGLOMERATE

Boulders, pebbles or shingle, set in fine-grained matrix, sometimes resembling coarse concrete. Derived from beaches, lakes and river deposits. Often found near deposits of sandstone and arkose. Highly compacted forms are cut and polished.

Texture Variable.
Color Dependent on type of rock.
Occurrence Worldwide.
Uses Aggregate, ornamental.

BRECCIA

Similar to conglomerate, but rock fragments are angular. The matrix is cemented by secondary silica or calcite. Derived from screes and fault zones and often found near conglomerate, arkose and sandstone.

Texture Fine grained matrix.
Color Varies with rock type.
Occurrence Worldwide.
Uses Aggregate, ornamental.

SANDSTONE

Sand in which the grains are cemented together by secondary silica or calcite. May be loosely cemented and soft, or well cemented and hard. Occurs as thick, stratified beds in sedimentary sequences, often showing current or dune bedding.

Texture Sandy.
Color Buff to brownish.
Occurrence Worldwide.
Uses Construction industry.

ARKOSE

Sandstone rich in feldspars. Bedding is sometimes present, but fossils are rare. It effervesces slightly in dilute hydrochloric acid, which indicates calcite cement. Derived from rapid weathering, transportation and deposition of granitic rocks.

Texture Medium or fine grained.
Color Buff, brownish-gray or pink.
Occurrence Worldwide.
Uses Building stone, millstones for grinding corn.

GREYWACKE

Poorly sorted, fine-grained or granular sandstone, formed at the bottom of ocean trenches bordering continents, by avalanches of submarine sediments. Occurs in association with black shales of deep sea origin. The color can be of various shades of dark gray to dark-greenish-gray. Varieties include feldspathic and lithic greywacke.

Texture Granular or fine-grained.
Color Dark gray.
Occurrence Worldwide.
Uses None of any importance.

LIMESTONE

Whitish compact rock that effervesces in dilute hydrochloric acid. Can be rich in fossils. The color can be white to yellowish, gray or black. Deposited in ancient seas by precipitation or by the accumulation of calcite-rich shells, coral reefs, around hot springs. Varieties include crystalline, crinoidal, pisolite and reef limestone.

Texture Coarse or fine-grained.
Color White, gray, black.
Occurrence Worldwide.
Uses Source of cement, building construction (locally), blackboard chalk.

SHALE

Splits easily into thin plates along well-defined planes parallel to the original stratification. Buff to various shades of gray in color with a fine-grained texture. Derived from ancient mud deposits, it occurs in most sedimentary sequences with fine sandstone and limestone.

Texture Fine-grained.
Color Buff, gray.
Occurrence Worldwide.
Uses Source of fossils.

CHALK

White porous rock that effervesces in dilute hydrochloric acid. Often contains bands of flint nodules and is rich in fossils. Composed mainly of calcium carbonate, with minor amounts of fine silt. Deposited in ancient seas by the accumulation of tests (tiny shells) of microscopic marine organisms.

Texture Fine-grained, earthy, crumbly.
Color White, yellowish, gray.
Occurrence UK, France, Denmark.
Uses As a source of cement.

SHELLY LIMESTONE

Highly fossiliferous rock which effervesces in dilute hydrochloric acid. Composed of broken and complete fossilized shells cemented by calcium carbonate. Represents a thick accumulation of marine shells and other calcite-rich organisms deposited in shallow water.

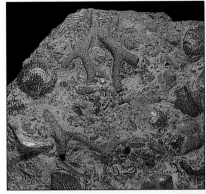

Texture Shelly.
Color Grayish-white, buff, yellowish-gray.
Occurrence Worldwide.
Uses Source of fossils.

DOLOMITE

Massive limestone that often contains small cavities. Sometimes associated with evaporite deposits of gypsum and halite. Composed of magnesium carbonate with small amounts of silica and other minerals. Often interbedded with calcite-rich limestones, but may form thick, massive deposits. It is sometimes known as magnesium limestone.

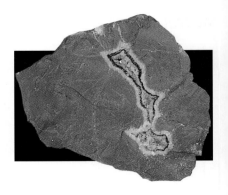

Texture Coarse or fine-grained.
Color Creamy white to pale brown.
Occurrence Worldwide.
Uses Aggregate.

COAL

A black rock that burns with a bright yellow flame, and is composed of highly compacted plant debris from the remains of ancient forests. It occurs mostly as thick beds in rocks of Carboniferous age. Varieties include cannel coal, coal and anthracite.

Texture Brittle.
Color Dull, earthy black, submetallic black.
Occurrence USA, southern Russia, Ukraine, UK, China, Africa.
Uses Domestic and industrial fuel.

SEPTARIAN NODULE

Ball-like structures, often enclosing shell fragments or other nuclei. Composed of sandstone or clay cemented by calcite or silica, the internal shrinkage cavities may be seen when the nodule is cut or broken. Color varies with white-yellow calcite filling the interior.

Texture Fine-grained.
Color Gray, buff, dark brown.
Occurrence Worldwide.
Uses Ornamental when cut or polished.

IGNEOUS ROCKS

GRANITE

Composed of feldspars and quartz, with accessory biotite and muscovite. The quartz appears as gray glassy grains. It is associated with fold mountains such as the Himalayas, Andes, Rockies and Appalachians. There are many varieties including, pegmatite, microgranite, oplite and orbicular.

Texture Granular, coarse-grained.
Color Black, white, silvery.
Occurrence Worldwide.
Uses Roadstone, building blocks. Poor fire resistance.

SYENITE

Composed of orthoclase and plagioclase, with small amounts of hornblende, mica, augite and magnetite. Nepheline and leucite may also be present. Generally found in magma chambers underlying trachytic volcanoes. Varieties include nepheline syenite, and anorthosite.

Texture Granular and coarse.
Color White, pinkish-gray, gray.
Occurrence Worldwide, but particularly in the Alps, Germany, Norway, Azores, Africa, Russia, USA.
Uses Building industry, superior to granite as it has fire-resisting properties.

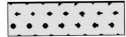

GRANODIORITE

Forms large intrusive masses in the roots
of mountain ranges and found in
association with granitic batholiths.
Composed of more plagioclase than
orthoclase, plus quartz, there are also
traces of botite, hornblende, apatite an
sphene.

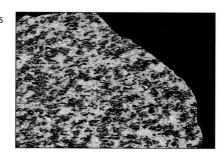

Texture Granular and coarse-grained.
Color Pale to medium gray.
Occurrence Worldwide, particularly
Scandinavia, Brazil, Canada, USA.
Uses Roadstone aggregate.

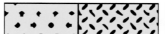

DIORITE

Granular though not particularly coarse,
hornblende crystals can give it the
appearance of a porphyritic texture.
Composed of more hornblende than
feldspar and more plagioclase than
orthoclase. The presence of quartz is
uncommon but if present, then the
variety is known as granodiorite.

Texture Granular.
Color Dark gray to black.
Occurrence Worldwide.
Uses Ornamental – capable of taking
a high polish.

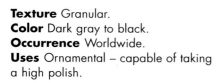

GABBRO

Composed mainly of pyroxene and plagioclase, olivine, iron ore and bronze-coloured biotite. Can be found as large sheets, often containing valuable ore deposits. There is a variety called Olivine, which is like gabbro, but also has olivine phenocrysts.

Texture Coarsely granular.
Color Dark gray to black.
Occurrence Scotland, Scandinavia, Canada, England, Germany, USA.
Uses Building industry, monumental as it takes a high polish, source of nickel, iron and copper ores.

PERIDOTITE

Made up almost entirely of small grains of olivine, or pyroxene may be present in appreciable amounts. Often brought to the surface from a great depth by volcanic activity. Varieties include dunite and picrite.

Texture Granular.
Color Olive green but weathers to dark ochre.
Occurrence Worldwide.
Uses A source of chromium, platinum, nickel and precious garnet. Diamonds are obtained from mica-rich peridotite in South Africa.

DOLERITE

Composed of large amounts of pyroxene and some plagioclase or equal amounts of both. Olivine is also often present, as well as grains of iron ore and bronze-coloured biolite. There is a variety called Olivine dolerite, which is dolerite, plus olivine phenocrysts.

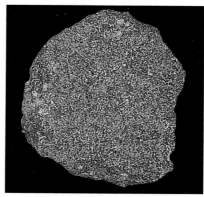

Texture Granular to fine-grained.
Color Medium gray to black.
Occurrence Worldwide, particularly Canada, UK, USA.
Uses Monumental, masonry, paving slabs, aggregate for roadstone.

RHYOLITE

Aphanitic to very fine-grained texture with the same composition as granite, but the crystals are too small to see without using a microscope. There is a variety known as spherulitic rhyolite, which contains rounded bodies of microcrystalline quartz and feldspar.

Texture Aphanitic to very fine-grained.
Color Buff to grayish, banded.
Occurrence Worldwide.
Uses Aggregate.

MICROSYENITE

Composed of orthoclase in greater amounts than plagioclase. The small amounts of hornblende, mica, augite and magnetite that are present can only be seen in thin sections with the aid of a microscope. An uncommon rock associated with syenite masses.

Texture Granular, fine-grained, aphanitic.
Color White to pinkish-gray.
Occurrence Worldwide, particularly in the Alps, Germany, Norway, Azores, Africa, Russia, USA.
Uses Aggregate.

ANDESITE

Composed of finely grained ground mass of plagioclase, with smaller amounts of hornblende, biotite and augite, which may occur as small phenocrysts. Found in lava flows and small intrusions associated with volcanic mountain ranges.

Texture Aphanitic, finely granular, porphyritic, flow-banded.
Color White to black, mostly gray.
Occurrence Abundant in continental collision zones, such as the Andes, Cascades, Carpathians, Indonesia, Japan and Pacific volcanic islands.
Uses Roadstone aggregates.

BASALT

Composed of pyroxene and plagioclase, olivine, iron ore and bronze-coloured biotite. A fine-grained equivalent of gabbro. Found in lava flows, sills and dykes associated with volcanoes. Varieties include olivine basalt and quartz basalt.

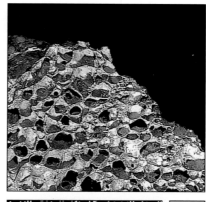

Texture Aphanitic.
Color Dark greenish-gray to black.
Occurrence Worldwide, particularly Canada, Greenland, India, Iceland Scotland, USA.
Uses Roadstone aggregate, source of iron ore, sapphires and native copper.

PUMICE

Composed principally of glass froth of granitic to granodioritic composition. Creamy white highly vesicular rock. Very low density. Found chiefly on rhyolitic to dacitic volcanoes.

Texture Vesicular.
Color Creamy white, turning pale brown when weathered.
Occurrence Worldwide.
Uses Abrasive, cleansing powders.

IGNEOUS ROCKS

PITCHSTONE

Composed of black opaque volcanic glass with the same composition as granite, syenite or granodiorite. Microscopic crystals of pyroxene may appear as white flecks while those of iron oxides give reddish colors. It originates from a rapidly chilled lava flow and is therefore always associated with volcanoes. Obsidian and vitrophyre are two varieties.

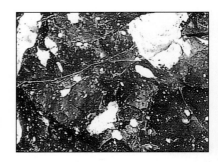

Texture Glassy.
Color Dull black.
Occurrence Worldwide.
Uses Aggregate.

ASH

Found in stratified beds of air-fall material ejected by volcanic eruptions, sometimes unstratified when formed from ash flows. Varieties include basaltic, trachytic and tuff. Composition depends on the source magma but mostly basaltic (black) to trachytic (white).

Texture Pyroclastic, consolidating to from hard volcanic tuff.
Color Pure white to black.
Occurrence Worldwide and always associated with with volcanoes.
Uses Prefabricated building blocks, road surfacing, abrasives.

IGNIMBRITE

A fine-grained to aphanitic, compact rock with parallel streaks or lenticles of black gass. Exclusively produced by violently explosive volcanos. There is a variety known as sillar, which is a poorly consolidated rock of the same origin as ignimbrite.

Texture Fine-grained, aphanitic.
Color Pale cream to brownish, dark red-brown.
Occurrence Worldwide.
Uses Local building construction, aggregate.

ECLOGITE

Generally coarse, pyroxene in which are set red garnets. Composed of omphacite, green hornblende and pyrope–alamandine garnet.
Kyanite and diamond sometimes occur.

Texture Granular.
Color Pistachio green when fresh, but mottled with red when weathered.
Occurrence As blocks in the 'blue ground' that fills diamond pipes in South Africa
Uses Scientific.

SLATE

Very fine-grained, foliated rocks that split into thin sheets. Sometimes containing well-formed pyrite crystals, and found in metamorphic environments. Composition of mica, quartz and other minerals. Found in areas of regionally metamorphosed shale or volcanic tuff.

Texture Slaty and very fine-grained.
Color Medium to dark gray, buff.
Occurrence Worldwide.
Uses Roofing sheets.

SCHIST

Mostly composed of biotite, muscovite and quartz and occasionally green chlorite, garnets staurolite and kyanite. Varieties include greenschist, mica schist, garnet mica schist, staurolite-kyanite schist, and amphibolite schist.

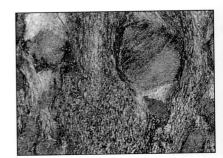

Texture Schistose with mineral grains that are platy or aligned.
Color Streaky, silvery, black, white or green.
Occurrence Worldwide.
Uses Source of minerals for collectors.

GNEISS

Coarse-grained rock, with darker varieties containing abundant feldspar. Composed mostly of feldspar, with mica, quartz, hornblende and garnet. Found in the roots of eroded fold mountain systems. Varieties depend on the source rock. Granite gneiss is the most common.

Texture Gneissose, coarse-grained.
Color Whitish to dark gray.
Occurrence Worldwide.
Uses Construction, ornamental, aggregate.

HORNFELS

Hard, compact rock that breaks into splintery fragments. Mineral content is variable. Hornfels is found in zones of contact metamorphism. Varieties include cordierite, andalusite, pyroxene and sillimanite.

Texture Hornfelsic and fine-grained.
Color Dark to medium gray.
Occurrence Worldwide.
Uses Aggregate.

METAMORPHIC ROCKS

QUARTZITE

Compact, very hard, finely grained rock, which breaks into sharp angular fragments. It is always associated with other sedimentary rocks. Composed of interlocking sand grains, often with silica cement.

Texture Granoblastic and very fine-grained.
Color White to creamy white.
Occurrence Worldwide.
Uses Aggregate, monumental.

MARBLE

Fine- to coarse-grained granoblastic that effervesces in dilute hydrochloric acid. Often banded with various colors and sometimes veined. Composed of calcium carbonate and found in zones of regionally metamorphosed limestone.

Texture Fine- to coarse-grained, granoblastic.
Color Variable, often streaky with light and dark patches.
O   rence Worldwide.
Uses Building and ornamental.

COPPER

Ductile, malleable with a metallic luster. It is opaque and dissolves in nitric acid. Native copper is usually of secondary origin in copper ore veins, sandstone, limestone, slate and near igneous rocks.

Crystal structure Isometric.
Color Copper-red.
Occurrence Russia, UK, Australia, Bolivia, Mexico, USA.
Uses Electrical conductor in wires, alloyed with tin (producing bronze) and zinc (producing brass).

SILVER

Malleable, ductile with a metallic luster. Silver is usually alloyed with gold or copper, and can be found as distorted crystals, reticulated and arborescent. Native silver is rare and is often associated with silver minerals.

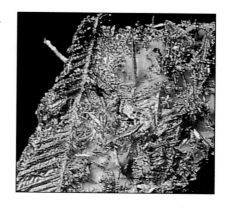

Crystal structure Isometric.
Color Silvery-white.
Occurrence Norway, Europe, USA, Australia, Chile, Mexico, Canada.
Uses Coinage, jewelry, ornaments, electronics.

NATIVE ELEMENTS & ALLOYS

GOLD

Malleable, with a metallic luster and is usually alloyed with silver. Ordinary gold is 10% silver, electrum is 38% silver, while other varieties contain up to 20% copper and palladium. Found mostly in quartz veins and placer deposits, but does occur in igneous, metamorphic and sedimentary rocks.

Crystal structure Isometric.
Color Deep gold-yellow, pale yellow.
Occurrence Worldwide.
Uses Monetary standard, jewelry, electronics, aircraft window screening.

SULPHUR

Ductile, melts and burns readily, giving off choking sulphur dioxide fumes. Transparent to translucent. Found mostly in sedimentary rocks, often clays, and associated with bitumen. Frequently found as small crystals around fumaroles on volcanoes.

Crystal structure Orthorhombic.
Color Bright yellow, red, yellow-gray.
Occurrence Sicily, USA.
Uses Making fireworks, gunpowder, sulphuric acid, insecticides vulcanizing rubber, medicines.

SPHALERITE

Resinous luster and color, transparent to translucent. Can occur in veins in most rocks, where it is associated with galena, pyrite, quartz and calcite.

Crystal structure Isometric.
Color Dull yellow-brown to black, greenish to white, colourless when pure.
Occurrence Romania, Italy, Spain, UK, Sweden, Mexico, Canada, USA.
Uses Principal ore of zinc.

CHALCOPYRATE

Similar to pyrite but deeper in color and often iridescent. Usually massive, brittle and soluble in nitric acid. It has a metallic luster and is opaque. Found in metalliferous veins in granites, gneisses and schists. Associated with bornite, malachite, azurite and quartz.

Crystal structure Isometric.
Color Tarnished brassy gold.
Occurrence Germany, Italy, France, UK, Spain, Sweden, South America, Namibia, USA, Australia.
Uses Principal ore of copper.

CINNABAR

Cinnabar yields globules of mercury metal when heated in a tube. It is transparent to opaque. Forms can be rhombohedral to tabular in habit, and it is granular and massive.

Crystal structure Hexagonal.
Color Cochineal red, brownish-red.
Occurrence Russia, Serbia, Slovakia, Italy, Bavaria, Spain, Peru, China, USA.
Uses Principal ore of mercury.

GALENA

Widespread in beds and veins due to hydrothermal action of mineralizing fluids. Found in limestones, dolomites, granites and other crystaline rocks and is often associated with sphalerite, pyrite, calcite and quartz.

Crystal structure Isometric.
Color Lead-gray, often silvery.
Occurrence France, Austria, Chile, UK, Peru, USA, Australia.
Uses Principal ore of lead and an important source of silver.

SULPHIDES

ORPIMENT

Often tinged with streaks of orange, it is flexible with a pearly to resinous luster. Forms can be massive and foliated, but the tiny crystals are difficult to see. Often associated with the equally poisonous orange-red realgar, arsenic sulphide.

Crystal structure Monoclinic.
Color Lemon yellow, medium yellow.
Occurrence Eastern Europe, Japan, USA.
Uses Pigment and removing hair from animal skins.

MOLYBDENITE

Soft, flexible with foliated scales and a greasy feel. When heated in a tube, it yields sulphurous fumes and a pale yellow sublimate. Found in granite pegmatites and quartz veins, syenites and gneisses as tabular prisms, often foliated and massive.

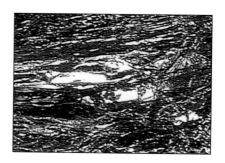

Crystal structure Hexagonal.
Color Silvery lead-gray.
Occurrence Norway, Australia, UK, Namibia, USA.
Uses Principal ore of molybdenum.

S

U

P

H

I

D

E

S

STIBNITE

When heated in a tube, it yields sulphur
dioxide and fumes of antimony oxide,
the latter condenses to from a white
powder. Metallic luster and has masses
of elongated crystals. Metastibnite, an
earthy reddish deposit, is a variety
found in the USA.

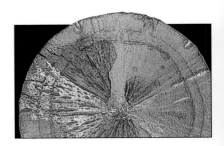

Crystal structure
Orthorhombic.
Color Gray.
Occurrence China,
Algeria, Mexico, Germany, Romania,
Italy, Borneo, Peru, and the USA.
Uses Principal source of antimony.

PYRITE

The most common sulphide with large
crystals produced in Italy. The crystals
are pyritohedron and cubic with a
greenish-black streak. It has a metallic
luster and is opaque.

Crystal system Isometric.
Color Pale brassy gold.
Occurrence Universal – the most
common sulphide.
Uses Source of gold and copper. Used
to produce sulphur, sulphuric acid and
iron sulphide.

ARSENOPYRITE

The most spinose member of the *Murex* genus, this shell is adorned with long, closed spines. The whorls are rounded and bulbous, bearing numerous spiral cords. The inner lip is expanded and raised adjacent to the columella.

Crystal structure Orthorhombic.
Color Gray.
Occurrence China, Algeria, Mexico, Germany, Romania, Italy, Borneo, Peru, and the USA.
Uses Principal source of antimony.

PROUSTITE

Found in hydrothermal silver veins and associated with galena and sphalerite. When heated in a closed tube, it fuses, and emits sulphurous fumes and leaves a white sublimate of arsenic trioxide.

Crystal structure Hexagonal.
Color Dark red to vermilion.
Occurrence Slovakia, Czech Republic, Germany. France, Chile, Mexico.
Uses Mineral collections.

OXIDES

AVENTURINE QUARTZ

Contains mica plates which give a sheen, with spangles of different colors. The brownish-red stones contain cubes of the mineral pyrite. Green aventurine contains green mica.

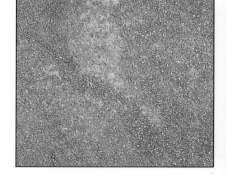

Crystal structure Trigonal.
Color Green, brownish-red, bluish-white and bluish-green.
Occurrence Brazil, India, Siberia, Tanzania.
Uses Ornamental objects and can be cut *en cabochon*.

JASPER

This is an impure variety of micro-crystalline quartz and consists of a network of interlocking quartz crystals. It is opaque. Varieties include riband, orbicular, bloodstone or heliotrope, plasma, hornstone, prase.

Crystal structure Trigonal.
Color Mixture of reds, browns, grayish-blues and greens.
Occurrence Worldwide.
Uses Fireplace surrounds, tables, facing materials, carvings, mosaics, inlays.

SARD, SARDONYX AND ONYX

Sard is the brownish-red variety of chalcedony. Sardonyx has straight bands of white together with bands of brownish-red sard. Onyx is made up of black and white bands and is similar to agate except that the bands are straight.

Crystal structure Trigonal.
Color Brownish-red, black.
Occurrence Brazil and Uruguay.
Uses Carved and polished for use as beads and cameos. Black onyx is often stained as natural black onyx is rare.

CHRYSOPRASE

This is a form of chalcedony which is translucent. It is usually cut and used as beads. Often imitated due to its rarity.

Crystal structure Trigonal.
Color Apple green.
Occurrence Bohemia, Australia.
Uses Beads, cut *en cabochon*.

O X I D E S

CARNELIAN

Also known as cornelian, it is the translucent red variety of chalcedony. The red color comes from the presence of iron oxides. Most commercial carnelian is stained chalcedony.

Crystal structure Trigonal.
Color Red.
Occurrence Brazil, China, Egypt, India, Columbia, Germany, Scotland, USA, Japan.
Uses Carved, cut or polished *en cabochon.*

CROCIDOLITE

Found in veins and pegmatites in granites and syenites. It has glistening fibrous crystals and a silky luster. Composed of masses of fibrous, thin prismatic crystals and can be either brittle or flexible.

Crystal structure Monoclinic.
Color Medium to pale blue, green.
Occurrence South Africa, Austria, UK, France, Bolivia, USA.
Uses Mineral collections.

OXIDES

BAUXITE

Formed by weathering of aluminium rocks under tropical conditions and deposited as a colloid. Amorphous and earthy-like masses. Sometimes occurs as fine grains.

Crystal structure Orthorhombic.
Color Red to yellow or white.
Occurrence France, Germany, Romania, Italy, Venezuela, USA.
Uses Principal ore of aluminium, also used in ceramics.

LIMONITE

Amorphous and earthy, Limonite is deposited near the surface after weathering of iron-rich minerals. Forms can be compact to stalactitic. Varieties include bog ore and clay-ironstone.

Structure Amorphous.
Color Deep ochreous yellow, brown, black.
Occurrence Worldwide, mainly in Canada and the USA.
Uses Pigments and iron ore.

RUTILE

Needle-like crystals in quartz crystals. Sometimes found in limestones where it has been deposited by mineralising fluids. Brittle with a metallic to adamantine luster. Often found as prismatic acicular crystals in quartz.

Crystal structure Tetragonal.
Color Coppery to reddish-brown.
Occurrence Austria, Switzerland, France, Norway, Australia, Brazil, USA.
Uses Ore of titanium.

CASSITERITE

Found mostly in granitic rocks and associated pegmatites and either nearly transparent or opaque. Varieties include tin stone, wood tin, toad's eye. Often associated with fluorite, apatite, topaz, and wolframite deposited by mineralising fluids.

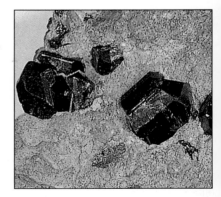

Crystal structure Tetragonal.
Color Brown to black.
Occurrence Malaysia, Indonesia, Bolivia, Congo, Mexico, England, USA.
Uses Principal ore of tin.

O X I D E S

CHROMITE

Occurs in peridotites and serpentine and is often associated with magnetite. It has a submetallic luster and is brittle

Crystal structure Isometric.
Color Black.
Occurrence The Urals, Austria, Germany, France, UK, South Africa, Iran, USA, Canada.
Uses Chromium ore, for hardening steel, chrome plating, chromium pigments.

PYROLUSITE

Occurs as a secondary ore deposit by circulating fluids, and is often found in clays and siltstones. The very pure form is called Polianite.

Crystal structure Orthorhombic.
Color Iron black to dark steel-gray.
Occurrence Brazil, Cuba, Germany, India, the Urals, USA.
Uses Ore of manganese, for colouring glass, in the preparation of chlorine, bromine and oxygen.

MAGNETITE

Heavy and magnetic, often with north and south poles. Found in most igneous rocks, particularly those of basic composition, black beach sands, serpentines and metamorphic rocks.

Crystal structure Isometric.
Color Black.
Occurrence Sweden, Norway, Siberia, Australia, Europe, Brazil, USA, Cuba, Canada.
Uses Iron ore.

HAEMATITE

There are several varieties: specularite, pencil ore, kidney ore, and clay ironstone. Tends to be brittle but is elastic in thin plates.

Crystal structure Hexagonal.
Color Metallic gray to earthy red.
Occurrence The Urals, Romania, Italy, Austria, Germany, Switzerland, France, Ascension Island, Brazil, USA, Canada.
Uses Principal ore of iron.

HALITE

The natural form of table salt and needs to be kept in a dry atmosphere. It has a vitreous luster and is brittle. A main constituent of seawater. Under pressure, the salt may flow upwards to produce huge salt domes at the surface.

Crystal structure Isometric.
Color Colorless, white to yellowish-brown, gray-blue.
Occurrence Worldwide.
Uses Principal source of common salt, preparation of sodium compounds, glass and soap.

FLUORITE

Occurs in a wide range of colors as cubes, often with a bevelled edge. Glows blue under ultraviolet light and has a vitreous luster. Blue John is a massive crystalline variety made up of curved bands of blue and purple.

Crystal structure Isometric.
Color Yellow, brown, green, blue, violet, pink, colorless.
Occurrence England, Switzerland, USA, Canada, Europe.
Uses Carved into vases and other decorative objects.

MALACHITE

Malachite is opaque and the shades of green color are due to the presence of copper. The compact monoclinic crystals are usually nodules with radiating bands. It is usually found intergrown with the blue mineral azurite or with turquoise and chrysocolla. When polished, the distinctive banding gives ornamental stone a silky luster.

Crystal structure Monoclinic.
Color Shades of green.
Occurrence Ural Mountains, USA, Africa.
Uses Jewelry, can be cut *en cabochon* as beads or carved.

AZURITE

Azurite is blue due to the presence of copper and is found as prismatic crystals forming radiating groups or spheres with a silky luster. An alternative name is chessylite and it is doubly refractive.

Crystal structure Monoclinic.
Color Blue.
Occurrence USA, Australia, Namibia, Romania, Siberia.
Uses Polished as stone or cut *en cabochon*.

RHODOCHROSITE

Rhombohedron crystals in mineral veins, where it occurs as a secondary mineral. Associated with lead and copper veins rich in manganese. A rare mineral.

Crystal structure Hexagonal.
Color Pale rose-red to dark red, yellowish.
Occurrence Romania, UK, Germany, USA.
Uses Mineral collections.

CERUSSITE

Cerussite is composed of white, striated elongated prismatic crystals, often in small stellate groups. Reacts to nitric acid. Its luster is adamantine It occurs in oxidized zones of lead-bearing veins, where lead ores have reacted with carbonate-rich water.

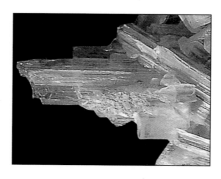

Crystal structure Orthorhombic.
Color Mostly white, greenish or gray.
Occurrence Siberia, Austria, Germany, France, Scotland, Tunisia, Namibia, Australia, USA.
Uses Lead ore.

ENSTATITE

This is one of the pyroxene minerals, with a chemical composition range of magnesium silicate to iron silicate. The more iron present, the darker the specimen. Too much iron makes the specimen almost opaque and too dark for faceting. The crystals are found as prisms.

Crystal structure Orthorhombic.
Color Gray.
Occurrence South Africa, Burma, Norway, USA.
Uses Cut *en cabochon* to show cat's eye effect.

RHODONITE

Rhodonite is mostly opaque to translucent and the color is due to the presence of manganese. It has distinct cleavage, uneven fracture and is brittle. It takes a good polish, makes an attractive decorative stone and is doubly refractive.

Crystal structure Triclinic.
Color Rose-red.
Occurrence Ural Mountains, Sweden, USA, Mexico, South Africa, Australia, England.
Uses Beads and cabochons for ornamental articles and as an inlay.

S I L I C A T E S

SERPENTINE

Massive serpentine can be divided into those stones that can be carved, and the softer types which are of little use as decorative stones. Varieties include bowenite, an alternative to jade, and williamsite which contains black inclusions.

Crystal structure Monoclinic.
Color Green, red, purple, brown, black, white.
Occurrence England, Wales, Scotland, Austria, France, Germany, South Africa, USA.
Uses Carved figurines.

KYANITE

Kyanite has lath-shapes crystals, and the hardness along the length is less than across the crystal. Often associated with staurolite in schists. Its luster is vitreous to pearly. Occurs in mica schists resulting from regional metamorphism, often in association with staurolite, garnet and corundum.

Crystal structure Orthorhombic.
Color Pale cerulean blue.
Occurrence Ural Mountains, Alps, USA.
Uses In refractory materials for furnaces and jewelry.

SILICATES

LEUCITE

Distinctive trapezhedral crystals in recent lavas of trachytic to phonlitic composition. Occurs in potassium-rich, silica-poor, igneous lavas, such as syenites and trachytes.

Crystal structure Isometric.
Color White to ash-white.
Occurrence Worldwide, particularly USA and Canada.
Uses Mineral collections.

MICROCLINE

Similar to orthoclase in appearance, but with a slightly lower specific gravity. Usually translucent and rarely opaque. Abundant in acid igneous rocks, such as granite.

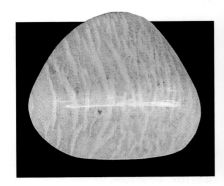

Crystal structure Triclinic.
Color Pale turquoise to whitish-yellow, pale brick red.
Occurrence Worldwide, particularly Ural Mountains, Italy, Madagascar, USA, Scandinavia.
Uses Jewelry, ornamental, porcelain manufacture.

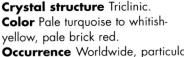

ANDULARIA

White to transparent crystals with a pearly appearance. Occurs in crystalline schists. It is the purest form of orthoclase found in granites, graitic gneisses and schists. It occurs in open druses and pegmatite veins, where it is associated with other granite minerals.

Crystal structure Monoclinic.
Color Clear to white.
Occurrence Switzerland, Austria, Italy.
Uses Mineral collections.

PLAGIOCLASE

Rhombic to tabular crystals in which the polysynthetic twinning may show as fine parallel striations on crystal faces. Present in almost all igneous and metamorphic rocks. Varieties include: albite, oligoclase, andesine, labradorite, bytownite and anorthite.

Crystal structure Triclinic.
Color White to grayish-blue or reddish.
Occurrence Worldwide.
Uses In porcelain manufacture, jewelry.

MUSCOVITE

An important component of many igneous and metamorphic rocks, especially acid igneous rocks, schists and gneisses. Occurs in granite pegmatites as large book-like masses. The plates are flexible and can be prised off with a knife blade or pin.

Crystal structure Monoclinic.
Color Colorless, pale brown, green, yellow.
Occurrence Worldwide.
Uses Electrical insulators, furnace and stove windows.

PHILOGOPITE

The plates are flexible and can be prised off with a knife blade or pin. Flakes often show a starlike figure in transmitted light. Occurs as a product of metamorphism and in serpentine, granular limestones and dolomites. Has a pearly, slighlty metallic luster.

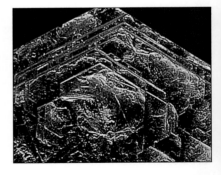

Crystal structure Monoclinic.
Color Coppery-brown, yellowish-brown.
Occurrence Romania, Switzerland, Italy, Scandinavia, Finland, Sri Lanka, Madagascar. USA, Canada.
Uses Mineral collections.

SILICATES

PREHNITE

Botryoidal or reniform masses of small tabular crystals. Often stalactitic or in radiating clusters. Occurs mostly as a secondary mineral in basic igneous rocks and gneisses.

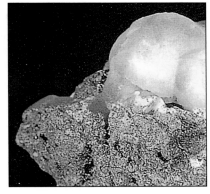

Crystal structure Orthorhombic.
Color Pale green to whitish-gray.
Occurrence Austria, Italy, Germany, France, UK, South Africa, USA.
Uses Mineral collections.

STILBITE

Waisted, tabular crystals filling cracks or lining cavities in basaltic lavas. Tabular crystals compounded into sheaflike aggregates. Has a vitreous to silky luster.

Crystal structure Monoclinic.
Color White to brownish-red.
Occurrence Iceland, UK, India, Canada, USA.
Uses Mineral collections.

S I L I C A T E S

BIOTITE

Biotite has shiny black tabular scales which are flexible and can easliy be prised off with a knife or pin. Splendent to submetallic luster. An important component of most igneous rocks, from granite to gabbro. Found in granite pegmatites as large book-like masses.

Crystal structure Monoclinic.
Color Black, greenish-black, brown.
Occurrence Worldwide.
Uses mineral collections.

AUGITE

An ovate and fairly fragile shell, it has unequal valves, the upper, or right, valve being more inflated. The depicted specimen clearly shows the characteristic extension of the hinge line. As in the case with most oysters, parts of the shell expand and crack when they are in a dry warm atmosphere.

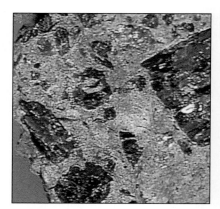

Crystal structure Monoclinic.
Color Green to brownish-black.
Occurrence Worldwide.
Uses An important rock-forming mineral in nature.

58

NEPHRITE

Made yup of an aggregate of fibrous crystals which form a very tough interlocking structure. It has a distinct absorption spectrum with a doublet in the red and a sharp line in the green. Through the Chelsea filter it looks green. Most early Chinese jade carvings are of nephrite.

Crystal structure Monoclinic.
Color Creamy to dark green.
Occurrence Worldwide.
Uses Carved or cut *en cabochon*.

·HORNBLENDE

Common mineral in igneous rocks, where it appears as black stubby, prismatic crystals. Vitreous, but often dull luster. Opaque. Varieties include; common hornblende, basaltic, riebeckite and asbestos. An important component of many igneous rocks. Found world-wide in igenous and metamorphic rocks.

Crystal structure Monoclinic.
Color Black, green-black, dark brown.
Occurrence Worldwide.
Uses Mineral collections.

APATITE

The crystals are fragile and tend to be transparent to opaque with a vitreous luster. Some lose their color when heated, others fluoresce a bright yellow under ultraviolet light. It has a characteristic absorption spectrum with intense lines due to rare-earth elements.

Crystal structure Hexagonal.
Color Colorless, yellow, green, blue or violet.
Occurrence Worldwide.
Uses Cut *en cabochon*, ornamental, collections.

PYROMORPHITE

Small, six-sided, prismatic crystals filling rock cavities in mineralized zones rich in lead. Has a resinous luster. A sporadic secondary mineral. Subtransparent to translucent.

Crystal structure Hexagonal.
Color Pale yellowish-green, brown, yellow.
Occurrence Germany, France, Spain, UK, Australia, USA.
Uses Source of lead.

MIMETITE

Six-sided crystals with flat terminations found in areas where there are lead-rich metalliferous veins. translucent and occasionally transparent. Campylite is a variety only found in the UK.

Crystal structure Hexagonal.
Color Yellow to yellowish-brown, orange, rarely white.
Occurrence Austria, Siberia, Czech Republic, Germany, UK, France, Namibia, Mexico, USA.
Uses Source of lead.

VANADINITE

Six-sided prismatic red to straw-coloured crystals associated with areas of secondary lead deposits. Resinous to adamantine luster. Rare mineral.

Crystal structure Hexagonal.
Color Shades of red to yellowish-brown.
Occurrence Mexico, Argentina, Ural Mountains, Austria, UK, Zaire, USA.
Uses Source of vanadium and lead.

GYPSUM

Soft enough to be scratched by a finger nail. When heated in an open tube, it gives off water. There is no reaction to acid. Varieties include selenite, satin spar and alabaster. Occurs as beds, sometimes massive, in sedimentary rocks, such as limestones, shales and clays.

Crystal structure Monoclinic.
Color White to pale gray, pinkish-red.
Occurrence UK, France, Russia, USA.
Uses Medical, wall plaster component, ornamental carvings made from alabaster.

BARYTES

High density tabular crystals. Also appeara as desert roses of radiating pale brown crystals. Occurs in veins and beds associated with ores of lead, copper, zinc and iron. It is associated with fluorite, quartz, calcite, dolomite and stibnite.

Crystal structure Orthorhombic.
Color White, greenish-white, pale brownish-red.
Occurrence Romania, France, Spain, England, USA, Czech Republic.
Uses Barium ore, refining sugar, drilling mud in the oil industry, barium meals for X-rays, as pigment in the paper industry.

CROCOITE

Elongated crystals, often in masses.
Adamantine to vitreous luster. Occurs
as secondary minerals deposited by
mineralising waters that have leached
lead from adjacent veins.

Crystal structure Monoclinic.
Color Pinkish-red to bright
saffron-coppery red.
Occurrence Ural Mountains, Russia,
Romania, Tasmania, the Philippines,
USA.
Uses Mineral collections.

WULFENITE

Usually as thin, tabular brownish-yellow
to orange crystals, associated with lead
ore. A secondary mineral, found in
upper zones rich in lead ore deposits.
Granular and compact forms also occur.
Subtransparent to translucent, with a
resinous to adamantine luster.

Crystal structure Tetragonal.
Color Bright orange to brownish-
yellow to brown.
Occurrence Eastern Europe, Austria,
Morocco, Congo, Australia, Mexico,
USA.
Uses Molybdenum ore.

Index

INDEX